Ash Dickinson is a multiple sl (including Edinburgh,
Cheltenham and BBC Radio
Canada, Australia, New Zea
the Czech Republic. He has l
throughout the UK, been
magazines and anthologies a
workshops. His first collecti
in 2012 by Burning Eye Book

www.ashdickinson.com

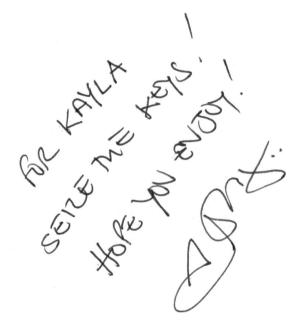

Strange Keys

Ash Dickinson

Burning Eye

This edition published by Burning Eye Books 2016

www.burningeye.co.uk
@burningeyebooks

Burning Eye Books
15 West Hill, Portishead, BS20 6LG

ISBN 978 1 90913 6 700

Strange Keys

CONTENTS

TIME SIGNATURE

she dances silently as the band packs up
eyes closed tightly
lightly picks up a foot
the last pulsing bass in the place tonight
her graceful figure contorts, cavorts
turns to its own time signature

catching herself in mirrored flashes
she smooths down her burnt umber dress
likes how it clings
pleased, impressed
the last stubborn pounds
burnt off at Zumba
back-to-back yoga classes
back on track, feeling younger
classic like Jackie Onassis

a man collecting glasses
stops/ for a second
and for a second
a chasm in him opens wide and yearns
as she glides seemingly free of movement
like watching the hour hand turn

METHOD POET

as Britain's foremost method poet
I immerse myself deeply
in any subject I tackle
I become one with my words
I disappear

for my revered epic
on barnacles
I attached myself
to the underside
of a peeling trawler
for four months
eating only ocean detritus
and phytoplankton

if you see me at times like these
and think it is me
it is not –
I have gone native

my life is essentially
dedication and sacrifice
striking a balance
between art and life

the first casualty
was my first wife
she didn't understand
that for me to understand
office supplies... fully
I had to lie in a cabinet
for close on a year
living, breathing, *being* a Post-it note
I was rewarded
with the four finest lines
ever written about stationery
– and still she left me

you grieve, you hurt like acid

and you move on
the poems keep you warm

wife number two I met on location
I'd been a plastic bag and the moon
and I'd been the sea
now I was researching
the climatic impact
of festival-goers on native plants
by attending Glastonbury
in the guise of a field poppy

she stooped
knelt over and smelt me
cradled me delicately
like I was newborn
I was so overcome
I had to break character

if you catch me off-guard
I will tell you she never
loved me more
than when I was a flower

people ask how we cope
all this time apart
but she understands this is art
this is what I must do

occasionally I return to our house
and find odd things there
unfamiliar hairs
pressed into the bedding
photos from our wedding
placed face-down on the mantelpiece
a sock, strange keys

and I think these are props
objects that I once was or one day may be

and I'm again clinging on like a barnacle
once more I'm all at sea

CASTLES MADE OF HAM

Mama Cass, singer with The Mamas & The Papas, was purported to have had one of the least rock 'n' roll deaths – choking on a ham sandwich. Hendrix: drugs. Morrison: drugs. Joplin: drugs and alcohol. Cass: ham.

butcher boils up in a corner
greasy drapes lava lamp lit
get him flying on his own corner
he'll tell you he can procure
the purest cured stuff this side of Parma
Bowie spun-out on a soiled sofa
off his face on gammon, legs askew
Page takes his acrid ham with eggs
diced, sliced neat with a bow
Lennon there, Dylan too, both like it smoked
take it like cannibals, great handfuls, choke it down
always a dolly bird or six lying around
paper-crowned, pulling pork, small talk
fed Moon like an emperor
dropping bacon bits into his open maw
medallion-studded, jaw to navel
more and more, more and more
and Mama Cass wants it intravenous
cut thin on doorstep bread
meat-raddled, they try to intervene
but she crams it in nonetheless
three mighty bites and Cass is dead
party over, smoked generation
time to get clean, go vegetarian

THE SMITHS CONCEIVE 'THERE IS A LIGHT THAT NEVER GOES OUT'

it wasn't environmental guilt, no one
spoke of carbon footprints back then
we just couldn't understand why
our electricity bills were so high
all we ever did was sit around
gloomily eating meat-free yoghurts
and emancipating the donkey
from Buckaroo

Morrissey could supplement his income
writing columns for the *NME*
but no one asks to read
the thoughts of the bass player
I had to get a second job
when we weren't gigging
I would sell biscuits door-to-door

to this day I can't look at a rich tea
without stifling a sob
hawking Hobnobs round Salford
bourbons at your beck and call

when people ask about
my biggest regret in music
it's that we never turned the TV set
off at the wall

BITCHES AND HOES

there you go again
with your bitches and hoes
I've seen what flows from your pen
I've caught your videos
the women in them barely wear a stitch
they've got no clothes
you flash the cash – so tastelessly rich
have them kneeling at your toes
fingers placed upon
your Abercrombie and Fitch
mouths posed for blows

when all you do is sing about female passivity
class women as pieces of ass
and wax about them physically
rap about how much on you they depend
how they cook/ and you look after them, control
what they spend/ pass them about your friends
it's no way to treat a muse
diss them, dismiss them
with a stream of abuse
would you address your mother like that, your sister
have your wife dress like that, your daughter
deny them independent thought
as though buying them goods
is them good and bought

you view women as accessories
– make them accessories to your crimes
you'd be better served getting singing lessons
spouting 'yo yo yo' a little less
and working harder on your rhymes
I object to your objectification
I wish to draw a white chalk line
around your need for women as decoration

bitches are dogs... dog
hoes are for digging... dig
now cut out bitches and hoes

hand them back their clothes
and pay some proper dues
you're always on about respect
show some, grow some
and some might find its way
to you

MY LIFE AS A POETRY LAPDOG

New Zealand immigration advised me
the only way I could remain in the country
was by sponsorship
I'm too old and unskilled for the normal channels
as for marrying in – they're on to me
someone's noticed how many small children look like me
right down to the beard
even the girls
wisely they wish to keep the population steady

why would they want me here anyway?
they know I'm only capable of writing poetry
who's going to sponsor a poet?
yet who can tell with people
who'd have thought one person let alone millions
would watch *Britain's Got Talent*
or give a career to Chris Tarrant
people are gullible
I remained buoyant

two days before my visa expires
I'm in a bistro uptown
eating lamb shanks
listening to Shabba Ranks
Chaka Demus and Pliers
I'm working on a poem called
'The Night My Aunt Caught Fire'
when a well-to-do glamour puss
wearing fake ocelot and fox fur ruff
sits down at my table and asks to see what I'm writing
– I'd just got to the part about my aunt igniting
she tells me it's not bad: 'there's not enough poetry
concerning relatives spontaneously combusting'
I say I've got another about a niece
who lost her front teeth crop dusting
she says she'd like to see it
anything further in a similar vein
I get an inkling this glamour puss
may be a smitten kitten when she orders champagne

smiles with teeth that despite her age
captivate and shame
make me hiss like a ventriloquist
to hide my own, arranged as crookedly
and yellowing as gravestones
thanking her profusely for the bubbly
she opines I'm remarkably well-behaved
for somebody so depraved
and I see she's not displeased
to find manners in a man
so like-mindedly diseased

she gives her name as Mary-Ann
she's a sexagenarian, a vegetarian
had one child by caesarean
and a husband who was a hairy 'un
and dead for decades
I've heard it said handsome's the phrase
for an attractive woman of such age
– it sounds an insult
holding her cigarette like a revolver
she says she normally smokes Dunhills
this one's a roller
it never drifts far from her lips
making her speech a series of frenzied spits
and long   dragged-out   draws
I envy this   considered   pause

hearing of my visa dilemma, she says softly
'I'm lonely and wealthy
rattle round a large house in the hills
trying to remain healthy – for what reason?
the kids are overseas, I rarely see them
I like to paint though I've little drive these days
live with me, I'll support your life's tale
there's room to write and regale
I'll sponsor you, if you stay'
and I think – ok
lived there for the next seven years
until the day she passed away

17

she didn't leave me the money
that wasn't the deal
we'd discussed it from the start
I'm a self-made man at heart
I never make much but it's mine
back in the UK it's like old times
scrabbling round for cash
as dirty as a water rat
having only two pennies to rub together
when rubbed they turn out to be chocolate
and melt in my palm like snow
it's the way life as a poet goes, I can't complain
no one gets into poetry for financial gain
one night I'm on stage retelling this story
at the end I'm approached by a man
requesting a little more info on Mary-Ann
I flesh out some detail
he tells me he's an art collector
that Mary-Ann was a painter of some repute
he has a lot of her early work
before she became a recluse
I knew she had talent
but I don't know art
being gallant, I hadn't probed
assuming her wealth payout
on her husband's early depart

the man asked, breathlessly
if I had any of her work
– it was what she left me
in her will, stills
the odd sketching, some etchings
preliminaries, sculptures in latex
plaster, some in alabaster
cost me a packet to ship them over
I said I had some pieces from installations
and then there were the paintings
lots and lots of paintings –
by this point he was close to fainting
turns out I was sitting on a fortune

weeks later, taking the art
from the loft with caution
the auction days away
I pause before a sculpture
imagine it taking shape, creating
building, base to nape
the angles, the considerations
picture the paintings emerging
from blank canvas, the deliberations –
when as if from nowhere
without frame or fanfare
I see a sketch of Mary-Ann herself
her teenage form, a self-portrait
drawn years before I was born
all the hope of the age in her eyes
and to my utter surprise I realise I'm crying
seven years, seven years I'd seen her every day
never was she more present

I move my bed up there
and each night I'm interpreted
cradled imperfect
perfumed in marble chalk
and daubed with light
each night I recline, composed
in position, stylised
still life – bittersweet juxtaposition
each night – awed, floored
formed, reformed, drawn, reborn
hushed and hued, brushed and blued
in the stillness, shaded
each night valued, revalued

and revalued

IF I MISS A COFFEE

my coffees are military precision
cup-two-three-four, cup-two-three-four
not a moment's indecision
must filter into their making
the kettle must twitch, flick its switch
as if conjured by a magician
for I'm waking – dreary, bleary
kitty-litter-mouthed
chanting a mantra of coffee coffee

comfortable dependable coffee
the first I know by name, it's an old flame
spun in its gentle steam
I hug the mug, its love handles
knowing like skin every curve and adorable blemish
we uncover, discover, one another at leisure
safe in the knowledge when this is over
another must follow instantly
or percolatedly
but never, fatally, belatedly

ka-BOOM! cup two fair rattles the room
it goes off by my third rib
a controlled explosion
I don't need the taste now but the hit
it is big-stakes big-screen bingo
I'm sitting on a line, breathless, down with the lingo
my heart thudding... eighty-eight... eighty-eight
two fat ladies
and the caller – herself a fat lady
starts to call eighty—

if I miss a coffee
I'm like a rhinoceros mother
who has discovered someone
trying to sell drugs to her kids

11.19, a third cup
always 11.19

a minute before
one minute more
the day could collapse/ in/ on/ me
this cup is straight up/ O/ C/ D
it isn't savoured like the first
or devoured like the second
it is as it is and always will be
like AC/DC
the dependent in my dependency

post-lunch, whipped, dipped
second troughs, second winds, tired and revived
on the ropes, it's the bean
that's been the beacon of hope
a frothy pep-talk to inspire this tiring dope
sip-sip, ding-ding, the phone's ring-ring ringing
I'm back in the swing
I'm coming out swinging

set, I give coffee the rest of the day off
it's done its job, it should rest up
but my, how slyly saviour becomes sinner
8.45 pm, the denouement of a late dinner
the cafetière comes around
easy chat on lavish three-piece
but I'm a caffeine gremlin –
I shouldn't be fed coffee after 8 pm
or I'll be popping steaming cocoons
of malevolence from my armpits
sure enough, I'm wired, fired, from just this hit
I have a strong desire to build a treehouse
with someone I've just met called Frank
then flutter my genitals at his wife
I'm guest-wrestling, gerbil-tormentingly wired
still there at 3 am, noticeably alone
not the least bit tired

morning, groaning, feeling I've been lying
on a satchel of hedgehogs

I'm in a heap – dreary, bleary
my reflection eyes me like I owe it money
scuffed, snuffed out
I paw the air for the only way
to hotwire today –

coffee
corpse-raising hallelujah-praising coffee
two sips and all comes good
the greatest drug in a mug there is
stellar guide
my better side
my dark roasted blood

BEFORE LIME STREET

moving on? I tried
but my heart and your heart are aligned
you're deep inside, inscribed
scratched into my psyche
slice me, cut through my skin
my blood is paraffin
coursing, shovelled in
to meet the heat and oxygen

rest a hand upon my chest
feel yourself there, silk-wrapping fibres
rising up through tips of hair
I need no outer ink, no external reminders
not when you're lines of melody
lines in movies
dizzying memories, crashing in from nowhere

this is not a eulogy
nor is this our time
these hands would not be tapping away at technology
mapping lines
if they could be holding, enfolding
wrapping your body into mine
dig in
dig in and believe
if the thought breathes
it can scorch bright
right across these desolate walls
thaw winter's wild and woolly moors
crash into the cheap stalls
fill every empty seat
with a rampant heart that skips like a needle as it beats

I've been wrecked, body-checked
felt the chills right through, at last
I sense the thinning of the snow
it makes me laugh when I hear it's the hope that kills you –
there are countless worse ways to go

ALIAS

I'd given myself an alias/ to distance myself/ from myself/ what's in a name after all/ but years and years of falling into patterns

the instant a hotel receptionist uses it/ I'm transformed/ reborn/ ...and the winner is....!

I'd birthed an elaborate backstory/ my grandfather, smuggled out of Nazi-occupied Austria in a vacuum cleaner (I had the make and model – the cement is detail)/ meets my grandmother in the Wirral/ transfixed by her eyes ('vast hopeful horizons')/ six days later they marry/ build an immense button empire/ sell it before the zip market explodes (millions would've been wiped)/ buy a zoo/ have my mother (I have her down better almost than I have myself) who, ultimately, has me, fathered by a travelling vacuum salesman (insert chuckle at the irony – the circle of life! existence out of the vacuum! etc.)/ opportunities to reveal the fullness of these worlds prove rare/ I'd taken to striking up conversations with strangers in bars: 'are you the grandson of a button magnate? no? I am' or 'don't you find hand-rearing a coatimundi transcendental...?' (it's always a coatimundi or a kinkajou/ a proboscis monkey – never the rookie mistake of lion or tiger)

my old identity haunted my edges like a car I'm towing/ have you ever towed a car then forgotten?/ looked in the mirror/ and thought – wow/ that guy is right up my backside!/ you put your foot down/ he only bloody goes and accelerates!/ the whisper campaign of my past is seldom far away

I'd read of a man with dissociative personality disorder/ six distinct personalities/ once he got in a lift that read 'maximum five persons' and had to take the stairs/ my given persona was enough weight on its own

why am I telling you this?/ aren't we all different people/ to different people?/ some invite intimacy/ with others there's a wall/ however minutely, though, aren't we all winging it?/ constructing to fit a scene?/ all the world's a stage, all the men and women merely audience/ a reinvention was the logical step/ I was on my way to becoming a concept

converging worlds muddy matters/ someone who knows Persona A introduces you to someone who knows Persona B/ I'd become adept at sidestepping/ relying on the depth/ the intricacies of the creation/ ultimately, though, all must go/ Persona C waits in the wings, gathering strength

I'd always made a better other man than a boyfriend/ the bit on the side/ small dynamic bursts/ pithy sound bites/ my capacity for love was finite/ the short rather than the feature/ the single, never the album/ I couldn't sustain a personality/ I didn't have the stomach for the padding/ all that filler – views on carpeting/ knowledge of interest rates/ the best place to buy brioche/ the minutiae/ such piffle sullied the first incarnation/ the alias is no less rounded but glitzier/ it has range/ as a work in progress it's hard to dispute/ however, like all personalities, avoid overexposure/ it's the ruination of the reality 'star'/ don't invite them into your home/ don't be caught arguing in Lidl, your hair all sixes and sevens/ pulling bits of chicken from your teeth/ your sweatpants out your cheeks/ retain mystique/ if you've ever eaten a lemon like it was a peach you'll know

one day the original me/ tainted/ outdated/ obsolete/ will be left like snake skin on a beach/ a papery imprint of what I'd been

and you will go and gently collect this up/ press it between the pages of a book/ carry it/ enthralled not by its otherworldliness but its tangibility/ recognise in it the me stripped of hardness and cold blood/ the one that just was/ you will trace along its form/ unpreening, caught-unaware Braille/ read the too-real me/ too vulnerable/ the me that had to die/ you will store it next to the owl pellet and the lamb's tail and look at it from time to time/ glory in its ordinariness/ and perhaps, for a moment, rue there wasn't more of it/ before heading out somewhere

I'll be in a square with a beer/ three empty chairs and a laptop/ cultivating some persona or other/ like a great artist convinced they're pulling off a masterstroke

THE RUNNING OF THE BULLFINCHES

they come to put their mettle to the test
high on testosterone, beating chests
a rite of passage, the running of the bullfinches

fiesta air curdling, swelling balconies, fear-sick
and frantic, claustrophobic, a mob of fevered feet
throb the street, dislodge ancient cobbles

each buck attired in white shirt, seeds
of fruit trees tucked inside red waistbands
fat balls bulge trousers

lined beside the weathered and the worn
saucer-eyed newbies fixate on skirmish scars
the returning torn, ears part-lost to inarguable bills

Valhalla bird call intimidating, surround sound
a growing crowing whistle, a few men
throw up into their hands

they tie the birds' wings (to more even the odds)
– no such restraint to bullet heads, wrestling masks
wall o' death motorcycle psychopaths

in the evening, it's the stillness that chills
arcades blood-scrubbed, raided for trophy feathers

hilltop bars sway with stories, songs of glory
each retelling more fraught, gory and long, hyperbole

hushed instantly, puffed-out chests turned pigeon
by thunderclaps of distant birdsong

and indelible visions/ of fire-red undercarriages

THE NEW YEAR'S EVE
NO ONE COULD LEAVE

the bells chime on BBC1
from an old set in the corner
another year gone, seen on its way
horse brasses, brassy boozers
whiskeys and wine
kisses from strangers
tipsy singalongs, Auld Lang Syne
too long, too short
the landlord calls time
on the busiest night of his year

only then do we notice the snow

shallow on arrival, flecks
specks party-popped the air
settling, sparsely, here and there
someone recalls a forecasted inch
a brushing soon turning to slush
– no one was prepared for this
drawn-back curtains shush the sloshed
draw gawkers, cork blurry slurry talkers

it's up past the window, several feet deep
thick and impenetrable, totems of sheep
we are children again, marvelling

someone tries the door – it's stuck
a lock-in! what luck!
shut in, snowed in, in a pub!
landlord – keep the drinks flowing!
keep the snow snowing!
not one soul's going
this New Year's Eve
check out whenever you like
but you won't ever leave

we joke about being here till spring
meet those not met, one happy family

carousing, singing, shut in
taps still spilling, revellers ever-willing

and they're snogging by the quiz machine
extra opportunities
we'll never be seen
again after tomorrow
we roar, guffaw, smooch and hug
time passes
passed glasses
some sleep in the snug
on the pool table
most just drink, a pale sun coming up

and nothing thaws
the door stuck fast

and we're getting peckish
the landlord – somewhat cranky
whips up some eggs but they don't stretch
that's ok, there's ale
food of kings in these remote dales
let's go again
and we do

but one locked-in night becomes two
and coupled promises are shown to be lies
they're fighting on the pool table
and all that's left to eat are scampi fries
and people are starting to smell
hangdog faces, party hair gone to hell
and the beer is running out
and the beer has run out
and we're afraid we might be here till spring
poor signals, no contactable lines
everyone's talking
of their other lives
and some are saying what if we don't survive

a third night arrives
even the drinkers can't face a drink now
just as well as the lager has gone
and the wine
and all the bottles but the sherry
and something blue covered in dust
the toilets no longer flush
the landlord looks like he might combust
no one is talking
numerous folk are sporting
bruises and scowls
some contemplate cannibalism
size you up in the television
howling, chanting
openly recanting
vegetarianism

overnight
that fourth night
it must have rained
over now
the snow outside the window pane
replaced by camera crews, twenty-four-hour news
how did it feel to be trapped
in a pub for three days, they laugh
the longest, most fantastic New Year's Eve!
but only haunted eyes shoot back
it wouldn't work on radio
but surely makes for great TV
smile, you're national celebrities!

someone get a word with the landlord!
but the landlord is nowhere to be seen
he's way out back
taking an axe
thwack, thwack, thwack
to his snow machine

21ST CENTURY BOY

friends tweet it's fine
friends tweet it's good
everybody says it's the UK's leading facial scrub
sm'mina extracts fortified with P-Zip Flinge 4 technology
to unblock the pores
whilst keeping the skin taut and springy
GQ tells me it's fine, tells me it's good
spend that much on toiletries my flat looks like a Superdrug
well, it's plain to see –
21st century dandy

move like a cat, make love like a woman
I like to hug/ I'm considerate enough to fake
when I'm not up to coming
I'm rubbish around the house
I know nothing about plumbing
– there are professionals for that
I can't change a fuse
but I do like a jaunty hat
I'm up with the news
I know birthdays, I'm not afraid to weep
I wear my ex-girlfriend's coat
it looks far better on me
I'm counting my intake, taking protein shakes
lifting weights, I'm getting healthy
I start each day with a reassuring selfie
21st century boy

groom/ groom/ groom-groom
groom/ groom/ groom/ -groom

friends post it's good
friends post it's fine
the latest Kate Hudson rom-com
which bombed on release but I've seen online
and I'm comfortable enough with my heterosexuality
to appreciate the character development
however slight and forced
even titter a little without remorse

I'm fine with discourse on *The Bell Jar*
and giving Jane Austen critical appraisal
it's just that I also love football
and would shave off all my locks
for one night with Megan Fox
I can go out with a girl and outlast her shopping
six hours not close to dropping
stopping for food, we both choose the lighter option
I'm happy with soy
I'm a 21st century boy

tough grizzled last century man doesn't understand
alpha ape at the bar, Carling in hand
he considers sweat man's one true scent
thinks guys' clothing should be at all times unobtrusive
and preferably flecked with dry cement
mouth agape, he knows only to assimilate
but his date rates me, whispers I'm great
slips me her number while he's trumping like thunder
ten minutes on he's still in my face, mocking my taste
I'm leaving the place, her arm round my waist, well

it's plain to see, she was meant for me
– only she's talking matrimony
it's just like rock 'n' roll – outdated / antiquated / a self-parody
kids – I wouldn't wish them on a worst enemy
baby / don't let it come between us
let's kick back with the Sunday papers
repeats of *Friends*, take a bath
I'll borrow moisturiser and your wax
and tonight we'll both be smooth in the sack
afterwards we'll crack open a beer
and discuss our emotions
last century man calls this 'queer' / 'girly' / ...worse
whatever would he think
if he knew I wrote verse?

THE LIBRARIAN

everything in its proper place
ordered, neat, concise
the librarian stands, enigmatic
her face a foreword
an inscrutable carapace
her shoes match her handbag
match her dress suit, precise
not one hair out of place
nothing trips off her tongue
sentences stride out with balletic grace
under cover – by which she is judged
she is a maze – red herrings
dead alleyways, as delicious a mystery
as Christie's archest twists
even her assistant, six years
at her side, doesn't know
where she goes at night
knows nothing of the hunter's eye
the violet nails recklessly applied
wildflower tats scaling a thigh
dancing in flats
to all hours; a passion
for single malts and outsider art
discreet meets, scattered clothes
karaoke boxes, scaled Munros
she gets classified and shelved, abridged
a skim – then into history they move on
no one stops to check her out
but you haven't read this one

HAIKU INTERLUDE I

gave you a shoulder
provided you with an ear
now I look quite odd

fun onion: funion
a new type of vegetable
makes you laugh, not cry

no ugly duckling
this swan wants to be a goose
he is trans-gander

HEART ATTACK AND VINYL

once/ music was vital –/ societal sculpture/ via a side of vinyl/
the best literate wordsmiths/ fusing lyrics to riffs/ could reshift,
reshape mass culture/ turn on commercial radio (click) – hear
the hiss/ 'all the hiss, all the time'/ 'the greatest hiss from your
generation and mine'/ white noise emanating from the stylus/
what's original enough to define us?/ sure, it's just pop, rock/
one shouldn't expect the intellect of Dostoyevsky or Nabokov/
but something written about the human condition/ more than
just boy meets girl/ girl meets boy on loop/ boy loses girl/ boy
sings about girl in quivering falsetto aimed at turning teens to
soup

has music run its course?/ pop – finally eaten itself/ endlessly
regurgitates the corpse/ as for rock – what pops into your head?/
consider classical music/ Beethoven, Mozart/ 200 years dead/
still touchstones of their art/ centuries on, someone'll pick up a
guitar/ rehash the Stones/ the Ramones/ GNR/ rock's moshed
its glass ceiling/ it's trodden water since before 'More Than A
Feeling'

r'n'b/ used to be/ rhythm and blues/ Aretha, Otis Redding/
punk made ya wanna kick somebody's head in/ and where is rap
heading?/ once politicised/ now a fantasy of self-mythology/
you're rapping 'I'm cooking like Delia Smith'/ because it rhymes
with 'spliff'/ this is not the clever simile you think it is/ you –
a big muscly tattooed gangster wannabe/ referencing someone
who bakes cakes/ and sits on the board at Norwich City

manufactured bands are nothing new/ but never has the media
so insisted they matter –/ the ludicrous importance paid to *The
X-Factor*/ give me some old folkie/ some old fogey with his self-
penned songs/ strong on imagery, integrity/ over the trumped-
up karaoke of Cowell/ his foul atrocities – music as units/ bands
as brands/ the bland covers/ music constructed for people who
aren't music lovers/ cobbled together without backbone, teeth,
heart or spleen/ I need more than auto-tune on repeat/ Eurotrash
groove/ vanilla-smooth production/ to engage my feet/ flex my
cortex/ kick-start my heartbeat

in the mainstream/ in the main/ it's been done/ that song
you're singing, it's been sung/ it's been strummed/ it's been
hummed/ I want to go to a gig with its edges on show/ feel the
mythologised spirit of rock 'n' roll/ Lady Gaga – we all ha-ha
when you dress up like a butcher's shop/ head to toe in rump
and chops/ but that butcher's hook is the only hook of yours
to lodge/ you've got to look to the classics/ search the fringes/
swim against the slew to reach the singers/ that feel it/ in their
marrow

Cream/ not just a band/ Rage Against The Machine/ not just a
band/ Radiohead/ not just a band/ Coldplay/ just a band

I'd like to believe my favourite song hasn't come along yet/ its
composer perhaps unborn/ musical thoughts unformed/ still on
the wish list – that first drum kit/ yet we've resurrected Tupac/
brought Jimi back/ your festival headliners are Joplin, Frank
and Sammy – fresh from mopping up at the Hologrammies/
Elvis isn't dead – he's a spectral projection above your head/
using smoke and mirrors we'll exhume your career/ the choice
is crystal clear: a dead Nina Simone/ or a live Chris Rea

maybe every art form has its glittering dawn/ its unmapped
lawn of pristine snow/ where one can go and plant a toe/ and
leave a mark so deep and formed others can only follow/ trek a
path ever more narrow and final/ round and round in decreasing
circles/ like the shallow grooves/ in worn-out vinyl

.YONE IS TELLING YOU

ne is telling you the next few years are crucial
aʊ ᵢis is the moment you split the bill
leave school full and never eat again
these years – they'll set you up
they'll define you
and what you do or don't do
is a direct result of them
but the classroom isn't the last room
in which you'll be educated
education is discovering archipelagos
stringing necklaces of burst pearls

and I wouldn't say university is overrated
but it's not the be-all / end-all
don't go and it's freefall
I never went / nor spent a day regretting
there's so much to be learnt from getting
out on the road early
and I know that sounds romanticised
very Kerouac
throw some stuff into a backpack
head off down a dusty track
into the sunset, never come back

– I'm not sure I did
that kid full of bluster
masking layers of insecurity and fear
headed to the other side of the world
and never reappeared
I didn't go to Cambridge
but I cycled the Golden Gate Bridge
never went to Oxford
never wore a graduating frock
but I climbed up, sat atop Ayers Rock
I jumped out an aeroplane
saw the sun rise again
from a balloon
I've had my invitations
to share my words with other nations

and I've gone
but I never attended graduation
never had a dissertation
due by the end of the week
and it never felt wrong

breathed in Hawaii / Fiji / Canada / Korea
gave poetry a go, made it into a career
I don't mean to crow
however it appears here
...fling your lids wide, march outside
take it all in, sup in the vision
your deepest broadest look
it's as valuable as any book
and more than television –
because you're participating

and if your gap year becomes two
becomes five
well, you've done it right
there are few jobs for life
all that life experience will stand you well
round out your puckishness
give you tales to tell

have a desire that never stops burning
a mind that never stops learning
we're on a rock that never stops turning
your time on it is short
there are jobs that pay good cash
but eat your hours
experiences that can't be bought
give me time over money every time
ephemera and the memories
of biography chased
a life sought

SHOWER GEL

my shower gel has written on it
in big letters, the words
'Peaceful and Soothing
Shower Gel'

this seems an odd boast
for a shower gel to make
certainly, though, it has never
given me a moment's trouble
if I look miserable when showering
it is tremendously comforting
saying things like 'c'mon, Ash
remember what a sexy life you lead'
before emitting a little bubble
that makes me go all giddy
and giggle like a toddler

and peaceful?
never have you seen
such a placid temperament
it successfully intervened
in the shampoo/conditioner riots
of two-thousand-nine
it is the Kofi Annan of wash-time
this manner runs in the family, it says
its great-grandfather shower gel
refused the Vietnam draft
fleeing instead to Canada
to preach peace
and make Canadians clean
and tingly

recently, in a hurry, half-asleep
I picked up, in a supermarket, by mistake
a 'Malevolent and Antagonising
Shower Gel'

I now only take baths

PAIRED UP PARED DOWN

your friends are paired up
so your friends are pared down
single, no wish to be
no one's free
to go into town
no one's around
'cause your friends are paired up
your friends are pared down
so how are you to meet that someone?

besides, you reek of desperation
something in your eyes ultra-keen
in your face they've all seen
it stains your lips
ten minutes to the club closing
you're panic-buying supplies for the apocalypse
chatting up everything from a beauty queen
to the fag machine
you can't go home
alone
it seems

frequently half your friends
or their other halves
wish to be this free
together too long with the wrong one
a see-you-teatime kiss in the kitchen
weeks without sex, a listless missionary position
one year past their three-year shelf life let go
cream sofa Saturday-arvo fighting sniping shutdown
do they long for some downtime
just them and their bits? perhaps
but in time they know what they'll miss
'cause their friends are paired up
their friends are pared down

and no one's getting any younger
you're becoming invisible
to those after which you hunger

twenty-five-year-olds will always be twenty-five years old
you can't compete with the taut physiques
anyway why rock the boat
when a gentle float's
what you're requiring
it's tiring

at parties it's couples
your couples aim you at the single ones
their couples aim the single ones at you
and this is the choice
if you can call it 'choice', not 'recourse'
of course in some way you're hanging on
for Kelly in Accounts' break-up and divorce
you've heard the whispers
but then you're again sifting the wreckage
of another shipwrecked marriage
it's not that you fall for the wrong women
but the right ones seem to be taken
if they're not good enough for someone else
they're not good enough for you – right?
am I mistaken?

pubbing alone, clubbing alone
'cause your friends are paired up
your friends are pared down
and you look your age today, oh boy
four thousand lines criss-cross your spidery brow
and though the lines are rather small
you had to count them all
you had to count them all

and all your lines are loaded
aiming for breezy bon mots
you drop bomb after bomb
watch them recoil and run
as each bomb explodes

and that's when you turn to internet dating

to get a feel of someone
before they get a feel of you
yeah, that's when you go online
'cause your friends are paired up
'cause your friends are pared down

GIVE THE PEOPLE WHAT THEY WANT

mine is the single shingle pebble
skimmed against the O2 tide
Miley Cyrus, tongue out
like a Jabba the Hutt in hot pants
I shout request after request
for her Hannah Montana back catalogue
'you can't out-twerk your past,' I holler
twice she shoots a look my way
that slab of uncooked gammon
lolling from her commodious gob
like a bored cobra
but mine is a forlorn bark
a ping-pong ball against a wall of sound

three days later, headlining a show
in the back room of a Suffolk boozer
I am thrown off my stride
for the third time in a minute
someone shouting out opening lines
calls for old poems of mine – doggerel
my late-teenage messianic phase
when I believed (...first believed?)
not only that I had the answers
to the world's ills
but these would be best
communicated in verse
and shared with a few friends
and a girl I liked at work

I squint past the bleed of the ceiling bulb
wide American grin, pint of Bishop's Finger
...man alive, it's Cyrus!
'do "Impaled Pigeons Bedevil My Soul",' she chides
my planned set list in tatters
but I do it, I do them all –
'The Irrepressible Solitude Of Kanwick XX3'
'Roadkill Bank Holiday'
'A Quantum Of Solace'
she thinks she's won

but she could learn from such professionalism
give the people what they want

fifteen minutes later
I leave the makeshift stage bloodied
but relieved Cyrus knew nothing
of my first big break
that of an apple-cheeked poet of eight
the titular lead in the Sunday morning
TV show, *Morgan Glamorgan*

I'd have been mortified
would surely have died
had she asked
for my big smash
'Bath-time With Nanny Nincompoop'

BIGGER VILLAINS

The Syrian political cartoonist Ali Farzat had his hands broken by
masked men, believed to be government militia. 'Break his arms so
they don't ever draw again,' one reportedly said. The controversy
over the Danish cartoonist who lampooned Muhammed was still
fresh in the mind. Then came the attack on Charlie Hebdo...

they broke his hands
pow! thwack! kerblam!!
snapped each finger, shaft to point
splintered, spilt the pigment
a toddler's messy scrawl

should have cut them off at the wrists
bust his nose, his toes
sprayed them up the wall
anything that can grip, manoeuvre a tip
a nostril can brandish a paintbrush
steer, subvert, set to work

were he left merely torso, brain and cock
chance will come one day by god or not
to colour in their eyeholes
in vivid piss

the blood spills vermillion
across the back seat
mixes with the federal blue
every pounding another seedling
another caption, slogan
another potent power potion

and you still think cartoons are for kids?
the real works of art don't
they know the currency of image
a picture's worth a thousand ugly words
there are bigger villains than in outer space
take up the pencil, put them in the shade
weaponise the page

don the paint-flecked cape
don't dampen the scream
tyranny thrives without criticism
highlight the fear, each propheteer
illustrate every hateful regime

FOOD PHOTOGRAPHER

photos on the menu really send you, appetise
the pictures making lies
of your lunch when it arrives
that's down to me
I'm a food click click click click photographer
I'm a yule click click click click log-rapher
I'm a hot click click click click dog-rapher
I serve up poetry in a shepherd's pie
can make a Pot Noodle smile
c'mon, sausage, give us your best side!
work it, broccoli, work it!

steaks shot at the height of their sizzle
dressings caught at the peak of their drizzle
linguini, autumn-ripe zucchini, rainbow fettuccine
quick snaps, click snaps
handy snaps of brandy snaps
candy up the menu flaps

my photos – you can taste them as I take them
smell them as I sell them
to the cookbooks and the magazines
the billboards and the TV screens
I can light a potato   just so
give it a halo, an appetising glow
I might shoot it again stood next to a drink
I might shoot it again if its eyes   blink

food doesn't fidget
it has no bad side in my hands
no ego, no rueful bad profile, no entourage
no dinner sulks to be airbrushed thinner
it's just the food and the illusion of mood
oranges and limes dressed up to the nines
super-sized, caramelised, the camera lies

whatever it takes to get an image right
foam stands in for nearly anything
polystyrene = chicken wings

and for spaghetti – string	click
and for spaghetti – string	click
and / it's / a / string film	click
it's a string film	click
it's a cling film	click
it's a cling film	click
it's a wrap	click click click click

I SOLD MY MEMORIES ON EBAY

I sold my memories on eBay
I have the docket itemising
the childhood seaside trips
the tastes, the twitch of Alison's lips
as we puckered up, closed in
to what I list, enticingly, as
'that dynamite first kiss'

I couldn't face the clutter
they were done, spent
repeats of repeats of repeats

a Mr Stephen Gray
of West Bromwich
was successful
he messaged to say they'd make
a nice Christmas present
for his mum

I think I packed them up happily
I don't remember

THE ANECDOTE

monstrously late/ a servant led me briskly down the hallway/
my flustered face tarnishing every dessert plate led away/
it wasn't my fault, though few juries would see it that way/
I collapse into the dining hall as if the walls were wet paper/
startling everyone

it is clear I have just interrupted The Greatest Anecdote Ever
Begun

expectant smiles are sliced away/ the air detonated/ all faces
warped, contorted/ as though I've just slaughtered the aged and
much-loved family mutt/ bringing his remains here between my
bloodied teeth, humming 'Hey Jude'

I attempt anecdotal resuscitation: '...so, you had an octopus
on your head?!' I say/ fanning this, the only line I heard, as if
hysterical repetition and laughing like a berk were the jaws of
life/ I am overworked bellows wheezing to a stop/ the cause of
a pause so vast flowers bloom and die

a wicker dolt stoked by shame, I burn for centuries/ when at last
the dread words came foretelling a moment passed/ they are flat
and act as snuffers/ the spurned anecdotalist (I am quite sure) is
my prospective father-in-law

all present/ a lynch mob of aunts, cousins, even Arabella/
interpret this remark as their own fresco of hell/ I am the collapse
of the dot-com boom/ the room is a crème brûlée, I'm the cold
blunt spoon

Arabella's father/ arm round my shoulder/ leads me away
toward the kitchen/ 'I gather you're a poet,' he says evenly/ I
nod/ 'I dabble,' he says. 'I once performed to the King of Jordan/
have you ever read for royalty?'/ I shake my head/ 'huh/ my
daughter said you had long hair/ I had long hair when I was your
age'/ I smile/ 'longer than yours, straighter too/ I modelled/
have you ever modelled?/ had the hip and fashionable knock
on your door to admire and copy your look?/ no?/ I shouldn't
worry, it soon gets tiresome...'

in the kitchen an octopus lies on a table like airless bagpipes/ 'put that on your head,' he says, motioning toward the rubbery lump/ 'wear it proudly like the grandest hat/ enter the study where everyone is convening for what I imagine to be coffee, brandy and lavish badmouthing of you/ and your night might be salvageable'/ the octopus is as purple as a new bruise/ nothing, except perhaps me at this moment, has ever looked more dead

my thoughts are shrieking falsettos graffitied inside my skull in splodgy ink/ they are: 1) how will a dead octopus on my head curry favour?/ 2) who are these people to be impressed and assuaged by cephalopod headgear?/ 3) a lady shark would rock this look at Ascot...

Arabella's father has blocked any escape – he is all arms/ the octopus, he signals/ am I asleep?/ I don't recall picking it up so how did the octopus get on my head?/ (later I'm told it slipped off initially/ splattered sickly on the parquet like a water balloon half-filled with custard)

Arabella's father props the door open with a limb/ I'm thinking deportment/ trying to channel the Brodie set/ sure this is how wet dreadlocks feel/ in the cruel mirror of a cooking pot I'm a defeated Sideshow Bob caught out by a flash flood/ adjacent, the study looms – another room wholly unprepared for me

in it they spin as one – the ghoulish aunts, jackal uncles/ I'm aiming for insouciant/ ...yeah, just another occasion sporting a dead octopus as a beret.../ flowers bloom, flowers die/ I'm on fire again like one of those candles that never actually blow out/ Happy Deathday Octopus Boy

a bicentennial hush – then the ceiling caves in/ two dozen sets of crystal gnashers twinkling in an orgy of mirth/ bellies of best pork rising and falling like wicked oceans/ 'Martin!' – a reproachful cry from someone: Arabella's mum/ twenties are given, taken/ rain down like ticker tape/ glasses clink ink ink

time does its death dance/ nothing bothers to bloom/ Arabella
ghosts limply across the room, a photo album her eternal chains:
'the first boy I ever brought home'/ a stuck-down Polaroid, a
rangy youth, a kipper tie – an actual kipper... it could've been a
mackerel, I don't know, the picture clarity wasn't brilliant/ boys,
men, ageing, thickening page on page/ always the same haunted
faraway look/ some poor sap wearing a badger as a cardigan/
eel camisole/ otter trousers

shake/ shake like a cyclone/ fling that rubbery sack of
humiliation across the room/ destroy everything/ storm out like
a hot-cheeked child/ leave Arabella forever, never return/ go –
go for a bus/ go like a Polaroid flash/ like a high-pitched laugh/
go before you process Martin's crowing call: 'I never thought
anyone would fall/ for the octopus...!'

THE BLACK AND THE BLOOD

it was easier than I imagined –
building a time machine

I had the time
waiting for the swelling to subside
the scarring to form or fade

I would get groceries delivered
keep my curtains drawn
home to the mirror
to the mess of blood and mash
and work on the time machine

March 2nd 1982
I was there

not in the delivery room
but later, as my assailant dozed
in an incubator

I don't know what I expected
a scalding sky ablaze
a vicious crack of thunder
tiny hours-old horns

but no – it was... he was... implausibly small
peaceful, helpless
so delicate you'd imagine a breath
would crack him

I held my breath

duly a woman came by
stood at my side
sobbed huge eggs of tears
a smile reflected, stretched
silly and wide
and I had to leave

better to get him when he was seven
alone
April 16th 1989
on his way home

stamp on his face

stamp on his face
until I no longer felt
this   obliterated
emptied of something
you can't refill

I followed him like a ravenous dog
raven-backed, stepped out
from behind a shadowed yew
cut across his path
this seven-year-old bastard

'do you like conkers?'
he said, talking, to me
asking a question, him, he
'got a new 'un
it's a fourteen-er
smashed Liam's to bits
you wanna see?'

he might have shown it, I don't know
I wasn't looking, I was gone, blitzed
those eager eyes, the chubby unsullied face

a face I knew only repellent
in unremitting flashbacks
an alley, a leap, a fist
thwacking shoes
bushwhacking arms
and that face
music-video-spliced

I've never been in a fight
I don't fight, I don't count that night
it takes two – I was just pulp and rags and terror

I returned to the park April 17th
with the biggest conker
I could find and had ever seen
I'd visited twenty-three autumns
on three continents and sixteen cities
and this was the one
a Canadian conker, it was enormous
it wouldn't emerge for seven more years
but I had it in my hand
I gave it to Timothy Michael Cartwright
on the morning of April 17th 1989
and watched his face explode
sensorial overload

he wasn't frightened of me, or suspicious
maybe kids of the eighties weren't
weren't yet told to be, strangers
being nice to them, for no reason
just to make someone feel... happy

I visited him – Tim – often
I must have done
for returning to that night
to the alley, to the minute
I'm not there, he's not there

a car approaches the spot, both of us in it
me in the passenger seat, laughing
playing with the radio

not far up ahead, it stops
I follow discreetly
careful not to be seen

Tim, the other me, we turn a corner
count out ten seconds, count it quickly

shout it loud until you drown
every anguished animal sound

running now, I take the corner
catch the final frame
a cavalcade of blows
a crumbled third figure buckled low
I note my face has none of the black and the blood

instead it is the face of a jackal
hooting, crazed
each draw-back of a boot a rush
a giddy hysteric howl, a thud
the cracking of ribs, hearts
it is the sound of time splitting
retching to a halt

HAIKU INTERLUDE II

is it socks or gloves
that make a suitable gift
for an octopus?

flowers, crisps, flowers
crisps, flowers, crisps, crisps, crisps, crisps
romancing the stoned

kestrel on its nest
egg warmed beneath feathered breast
raptor in rapture

STALK THIS WAY

I want you to be my stalker
you don't need to be much of a talker
low late-night hurrh-hurrh-hurrh
down the receiver
simply suffices
as does an appetite for peculiar vices
and spending the night hunched up in hawthorn

profess to be my lover, my mother, a dotty old aunt
confess to be my closest friend
the inspiration for every poem I've ever penned
be relentless
spring from twitchells and snickets
at three minutes past midnight and spook me senseless
interrupt my sleep with window-tossed gravel
when finally I brave a peek
I hope to see my name spelt out in burning Ford Mondeos

can you handle rummaging through refuse?
the sodden tissue/ nail clipping/ fruit peeling
discarded hair DNA of my makeup
or my flatmates'
depending on your luck
or success rate
you might find a bank statement
and steal my identity
you have my blessing
go ahead – take plenty
anyone spending hours
up to their waist
in waste
deserves reward

pocket my lint, furtively, for a start
wear it in a locket hanging down to your heart
upload photos to Facebook
seemingly took with a telephoto lens
me with friends or mid-shave
leant over a basin in my underwear

looking slovenly and bed-headed
Photoshop us on holiday together
hand-in-hand, the bone-white sand
the immaculate weather
my head pasted onto the body
of what looks a lot like Bill Oddie

experience is desirable
do you find Jeremy Paxman admirable?
have years of bothering him
swiping his newspaper
or exposing yourself at his village fête?
if so – great!
maybe you've created a life-size effigy of Glenn Hoddle
become bored with his wheelbarrow jaw
and wish to switch to a younger model
if so, this opening's for you

I want you to be the type of person
market researchers cross the road to avoid
could you bring CDs to my gigs
chosen especially for me?
rubbish ones from petrol stations
like *30 Bullfighting Classics*
or *The Azerbaijan State Orchestra
Play The Greatest Hits Of Nelly Furtado*
there must be freebies
from the *Daily Mail* in cardboard sleeves
including at least one like Michael Palin's
Pole To Pole that's not even music
I want your favourite band to be a Bon Jovi tribute
that sometimes plays your local Yates's
your second favourite band / must be / Bon Jovi

poison my goldfish
kidnap my old Geography teacher
take a pot-shot at Reagan
to prove your infatuation
don't let his already being dead stand in your way

58

are you comfortable posting love notes
written in the blood of flies through my letterbox?
if so, don't delay
I want you – yes, you – to be my stalker
if you've the inclination and time
to follow me around and build a shrine
apply herein
I'm looking for a one-in-a-million
bunny-boiling fruitcake loose screw
because I'm simply not complete
without you

BERYL'S GARDEN

for forty-three years
he has manufactured
small wooden signs
that spike into soil
each bears a simple
carved floral scene
and the words 'Beryl's Garden'
– he is highly specialised

too specialised, thinks his wife
contemplating what new to do
with packet rice, another night
of white sliced bread
no-frills canned veg
if only he'd make some Karens
an Emily now and again, an Anne

he recalls the business boom of the seventies
but only occasionally bemoans
the lack of latter-day Beryls
besides, he tells his wife
he is too long in the tooth
to craft Rachels, Ruths

moving aside another stack
of unsold plaques
to create room for his mug
he leans back
in his plastic workshop chair
his gaze drifting away from his tools
and out across the dead azaleas

his flawless bride
fine-lined as etched crystal
hair like silver streamers
cascading slim shoulders
her fertile heart had tended
to his beds, bloomed
in every room, dug him
thought his work something

a starling makes use of the garden
shakes its iridescent head in frost
he picks up a skew, turns it
remembers these hands shaping
wonderlands on the tan of her back
softly lathing palm-flat a thigh bone

she is in the kitchen, on the phone
on the wine, haloed by a hanging bulb
he can make her out through the weeds
probably talking to her sister
more beautiful than ever
where have forty-three years gone?

somehow, at some time
love left the tongue
but in him only deepens
strong and unflinching
cut as though by chisel
a perennial summer song
ingrained, his always
his only one
Beryl

BLOOD RED CARPET

Russell Crowe's double-breasted
but it's not his chest in the firing line
who got you dressed? Prada, Versace?
whose line is it anyway?
not yours, not this time
you've no dialogue tonight
they've got you stitched up tight
demigoddesses scared mortal
more Demi more Julianne more
on the blood red carpet

so Mr Hanks, Mr Pitt!

are you going to win?

what are you next starring in?

yeah, we got the shot of you

top to chin, walk right in

we won't stop you again

you could be dressed in a bin liner

we don't give a shit

capture Cameron's errant eyeliner

Megan's bare back, zoom in

on Jen's zit, Kate's rack

print it off, rack up a viral hit

but first we need you to pirouette

we haven't seen enough skin just yet

we want you from all angles

make face, dangle further whatever dangles

you know what we want, you know

imagine you didn't carve out

a successful career

and had to resort to porno

that's it, act it out

this ain't theatre, love, it's panto

spill

they'll rate your style, face, figure
debate it endlessly – have you got bigger?
shine the flashlights hot in your eyes
you've won tonight if you've accessorised
two hours in make-up, necessarily glamorised
you're the best actor of your generation
mesmerising, venerated
but they don't even know
in what category you've been nominated
your film, no one here's seen it
you're carpeted, pet
uncredited

DUCK FEATHER

a single feather
poked through my jacket
so I pulled at it
pulled and pulled, pulled and pulled
until out came a duck
an entire/ bemused/ duck

we stared at each other
dumbstruck

the duck was spotlessly white
as though bleached
each square inch startlingly pure
except for – a single/ brown/ hair
I paused – then pulled there
pulled and pulled, pulled
and pulled, lo and behold
a man emerged, six foot
head to toe, thirteen stone

he was smartly attired
sharp-suited, tailored
top label, immaculate
save for a single/ blond/ speck
on the lapel
what the heck – I pulled at it
pulled and pulled, pulled
and pulled until
with one big final pull
a woman emerged
early thirties/ professional

the man, the woman and the duck
gave one another a sideways look
then leant in towards me
and began to pluck
pulling, pulling
pulling and pulling
until finally
out came
this poem

GUEVARA TEE

Guevara tee
under your work whites

his image adorns
your office cubicle

if the revolution ever comes
you'll find some filing to do

another cliChe

SPOTIFIED KIPLING

'do you know roses are red?!'
not all of them, I say
but I'm being facetious
it's Saturday night so of course I'm doing covers
but if one more of these... fuckers
requests 'If'
this microphone's going through their skull

vodka/Red Bull hour
daft sods on the pull hour
two thirds down the set-hour
I try to sneak in one of my own
but the floor thins
and I know I need some WH Auden to win them back
the promoter gives me a fat look
that says 'no "Glass Coffin"'
and I smile with vomit lips
through another of Shakespeare's sonnets
and think about the money

tonight's that rare night I'm not paid in beer
I'm pocketing my fee when the manager appears
whispers in my ear
says, 'we like what you do – just don't do it here
no one wants anything they've not heard before
familiarity is reassuring, don't you understand?
people want to mouth along with the stanzas
they've learnt by rote
they want nothing you wrote
unless you happen to be the ghost of Seamus
or Dylan Thomas, become famous, fulfil your promise'

was it ever thus?
is it any wonder the pool of originality seems spit-thin?
it's original sin
the path to fame ought to be the Plath to fame
even if it means doing yourself in
but if you want to play your own stuff
they say go busk for a penny, son

inside the DJ just spins Spotified Kipling
while hot young things karaoke Tennyson
and poetry on TV – it's just for the ratings, man
a popularity contest
vote in whoever's the prettiest
don't let them write their own ditties
and hey, a newly-conceived couplet
can't compete anyway
with plastic titties
and an appetite for the classics

so we're left alone in a grotty attic
simply to regale one another
proudly resilient – broke, sure
but glad for the break
from another shitty cover

MOTHS

how can one so full of moths
speak of butterflies?

recognise the near-imperceptible
flutter of tiny knives
beat on the off-beat
deep inside

weigh day's easy pleasures
against the frenzied night
and welcome in the light
bask in soft colours
painted eyes hooded blind

there are hearts
that get broken
if you leave them wide open
hide your markings in a prayer
and you'll never again feel the air
or describe the sky

never captured, still enmeshed
freedom's a sly net
a specious tack, spear one stealthily
straight through the back

what a thing to crave...
what are butterflies anyway
but bugs with wings

STAR WARS IN THREE MINUTES

a long time ago
in a galaxy far, far away
from CGI rethinks
and technically-after-
but-mercifully-before
Jar Jar Binks

a star destroyer
long, black and ominous
like Vader's cloak
Leia uploads a YouTube video
Obi-Wan, you're my only hope
stopping
she wonders if it'll get more hits
than the one of Jabba body-popping
R2, 3PO in a pod for hours
land in sand, get separated
get jumped by jawas
bought by Uncle Owen and Aunt Beru
twin suns, a daydreaming nephew
cue wistful music and a bad transistor
cut to Luke getting the hots for his sister
R2 does a runner
so too the tusken raiders
they'll be back – and in greater number
Ben shuffling on looking simply like a coat
(there's more of this to come, you know)
Luke, you must learn the ways of the force
I can't, I've got to get home or I'll be in big trouble
arrives home... *ah, my relatives are smouldering rubble*
ok, set a course

for Mos Eisley
a more wretched hive of scum and villainy
there isn't/ outside of Leeds
greed is good, Greedo is not
Han takes him out with one low shot
that's right – Han Solo, and Chewbacca
Harrison Ford in the role that made him

and a seven-foot-tall English actor
dressed in carpet chic
hanging out in a bar
that looks like Dresscodes Nightclub in Mansfield
only with less freaks
he's got the Millennium Falcon
and is taking Luke, the old man and the droids to Alderaan
but grrr! it's just been pulverised by the Empire!
the sat nav says: *you've reached your destination*
but it's just rock fragments, obliterated Burger Kings
...and a massive space station
of course they try to flee the scene
but – *irony*, thinks Luke
you try to escape the farming industry
only to be caught in a tractor beam
then a trash compactor
and that only after
you've dressed up as a stormtrooper
and rescued a future queen
and just when things seem ok
Obi-Wan becomes a coat again
struck down by Vader's 'saber
the Sith Lord pokes it with a foot
then picks it up, puts it in the recycling
it's found shortly by the Death Star's night porter
thinks, *ooh, it's nice thick cloth*
will come in handy/ should there be a sequel
on the ice planet Hoth

our heroes escape
though I should mention the fire-fight scrape
and the palpable sexual tension
oddly it's Han that repeatedly calls Leia sister
and in real life he's old enough to be father to Carrie Fisher
but I digress
cut to hyperspace
a homing beacon tracking the rebel base
who counter-analyse plans to defeat them
and it's a countdown

I'll have a consonant – T
a vowel – I
another vowel – E
a Y, an X – and next
the rebel force are in the sky
scything along the Death Star's trench
getting shot up until it looks like Luke's by himself
the Empire getting way too close for the rebels' health
if only Han hadn't scuttled off when he did
hang on
...*great shot, kid!*
Luke's aimed a torpedo
Vader's spinning like disco
the Death Star lit up like a glitter ball
medals to all necks but the wookiee's
Han wondering if he can pawn his
one-nil to the rebels
cue John Williams
roll closing titles

EUSTON, WE HAVE A PROBLEM

St Pancras station/ Betjeman waiting/ hanging on to his hat/
nothing nearing to knock it back/ desolate platform/ wrong
leaves on the track/ stood like statues/ signalling problems/
a crew lacked/ the perfect storm/ high winds roaring forth/
seventeen minutes late – escaped puma, Chessington North

at Waterloo, an advert – London to Sydney £700 flight/ right
on!/ turn up on the day, the train's that much to go to Brighton/
anyway there's no point alighting/ we've run out of track/
thieves have taken it up/ sold it for scrap/ there's no going
back/ they're coming up behind/ lifting it up as we pass/ five
carriages of islanded metal/ marooned in grass

fleece peak commuter time/ inflated fares 4 to 7/ 6am and 9/
got you held to ransom/ more hair dye for Branson/ Virgin on
the immoral/ packed in like cattle/ half the comfort, twice the
price/ year on year, another hike/ cross the country quicker on
a Boris bike

fifty pee at the station to spend a penny/ my wallet's moths/ I
don't have any/ tax on the bladder, over-inflation/ price all bar
fat-cat controllers out of urination

still reeling from Beeching/ Berlin Walled families/ cut-off
communities/ cuts far-reaching – unlike the lines/ parts of
Devon accessible as the Amazon/ tribes in its farthest-flung
places never seen a Cornish face/ never eaten a hamburger/
don't know its taste/ never read a newspaper/ branch lines
long overgrown/ locals know of Victoria/ think she's still on the
throne

at last onboard/ a myriad of notices you can't ignore/ rebuke
and inform/ keep hold of your seat reservation/ a secondary
piece of information we almost certainly could have printed
on the main ticket/ another thing to lose and invalidate it/ like
an airport terminal, start your journey feeling like a criminal/
are you sitting comfortably?/ then we haven't done our jobs
properly

the buffet car is now open / serving hot and cold snacks / hot and cold drinks / which we will detail over the next four minutes in case you have no idea a hot drink could mean coffee / describe what a sandwich is in case you've had a lobotomy / crew leaders overegging lines / all we need know is / you're open for business / and your week's pay will get you two small wines

please note / only first-class ticket holders may sit in the first-class section / you may have paid a small fortune for a short connection but you still can't have a slightly more comfortable chair / it's empty in there / while they're stood up in carriage B / it's carnage at Ely / delays every which way / eight deep on the platform / true to form they're slow to inform of cancellations / what's the fuss? – we're laying on a replacement bus / arrive sooner tramping fields with a compass / the late arrival into Earley passes without remark

a service for the people / to ease our lives / but we've been sold out / privatised / don't need a trainspotter's eyes / to see other types of green among the leaves / a little greed / a little greener / nothing environmental in monumental bonuses, a new Beamer / staff costs / rolling stock / and take the rest / line the nest

at some point, esteemed praise, steam heydays curved away / metre and rhyme uncoupled / from hanging baskets at chocolate-box stations / folk in their Sunday best dress, a diverging path / Betjeman mute, waiting, delayed / twirling his moustache, the train operator laughs / we're tied to the tracks / carriage jumping, buckling / white-knuckled, we brace for the crash

do kids still dream of driving trains? / no passages for passengers / romanticised dispatches of a bygone age / no longer eulogised / hard facts in the *Financial Times* / a network of broken synapses / verse untravelled to the page / in the shadowless unclouded glare / deep blue above us fades to whiteness / defunct branch lines / blank lines for writers

RUNNING LATE FOR A
PUNCTUALITY SEMINAR

running late for a punctuality seminar
eight minutes to make an eleven-minute journey
I could run it in six but then I'd be early
and I think punctuality
is actually
about the dot

down, out, on the hot streets in my best boots
seconds, they'd be most people's thirds
their hollow heels ricochet call-and-response gunfire
to the unsuspecting residents their sudden appearance
simulates the ravaged heartland of Iraq
the castanet clack of a pterodactyl's snap
the final argumentative words signalling no way back
da-dack/ da-dack/ da-dack

taped to a pole, a sign advertises a yard sale
I have a yard
it used to be 0.96 metres
but the metric scale hit me hard
in it I mainly grow concrete
it feels manly and rugged beneath my feet
sure, to most it's hardly beautiful – not me
the beauty of slabs, see
is they're hardy perennial

you can increase your arm span
four millimetres a year reading broadsheet newspapers
there's a chartered surveyor in Cheam
taken the *Guardian* every day since the age of fifteen
has the reach of an albatross, arms fully unfurled
if he so chose he could be featherweight champion of the world
stand far enough away from his tabloid-reading opponent –
span that of a pigeon
no connecting jabs will ever come his way
even if he doesn't knock him out, he'd get the decision

further down the street, his eyes watery-weak
knee-deep all last night in Jacob's Creek
a man gropes for speech
I've been there, buddy
it's why I take my meds every day of the week
I know you shouldn't mix 'em with alcohol
but I'd rather swig wine with a pill
and if I can't drink, truly I'm ill

I can trace most of my problems back to childhood
were it not for candy cigarettes I wouldn't be a thirty-a-day man now
and chewy beer bottles are the reason my liver
was recently described by *Where to Stay* magazine
as 'spacious and affordable'

I go in sweet shops today
it's all gummy syringes
and chop-your-own sherbet
I know it'll end in tears
I once voiced my concerns to a shopkeeper
but he just spelt out 'GET STUFFED' on the counter
in scented alphabet letters

I recall jelly always being lime, now it's vodka

toys have gone the other way
as a kid we had Lego Technics
now there's Lego Ethics
you still build the same stuff
but you're invited to question
whether it's environmentally responsible
constructing a sports car

I could use it now, that car
running late
for a punctuality seminar

DRAWN TO A VASE

drawn to a vase, its moons, its stars
night roars, echoes out late-night bars
oh, to lift it, turn weight in hand
succumb to some innate command
smash glass, swift and fast, incite scars

Russian treasure, whispers of tsars?
all cried out, pried out by crowbars?
glossed, embossed, lost to a seized land?
drawn to a vase

what price Jupiter? what price Mars?
what price, what prize, such objet d'art?
Saturn? gild pattern fine as sand
and lo, see it filled, as I stand
held, cut, displayed, half-lit by cars
drawn to a vase

HAIKU INTERLUDE III

I watch what I eat
might miss my mouth otherwise
put cake in my eye

trapped in a tower
Rapunzel lets down her hair
it holds – Timotei

I'm down with the kids
particularly the emos
they seem the most down

SUMMER BIRD

This was written in the run-up to the Scottish independence referendum of 2014 – a response to a particular instance of online jingoism; it doesn't have in its sights the many people who put out reasoned, passionate arguments for both sides. I've spent similar amounts of time in Scotland and England over the last ten years, still live and work in both. England-born, Edinburgh-romanced, I refer to myself as British. I started out pro-union yet found myself increasingly sympathising with the Yes vote. I don't think either campaign, however, made much reference to the many nationalities that call Scotland home. Scotland isn't only Scots...

whichever way the vote goes
we have our independence
your posts go up between us
partisan rhetoric bricking up
sides, north–south divides
nationalistic pride
entitlement that somehow
the arterial closes pump
your blood that bit faster
to the heart of Midlothian
the battle for hearts
and minds has begun

your voice
may have a deeper burr
it may reflect a register
matured in oak, burnished
in iron and frost smoke
coming off northern lochs
it is not this hotchpotch
of points south of Scots
but cuckoo tongues speak
pride of Morningside, affinity
of Leith, Newtown streets
parts affection reaches
in which colours are placed
corners of bars, leafy parks
that feel ours

but some flags will never
be wholly accepted
differently accented
questions will be asked

you're not from round here
you've not the vernacular
nations are for natives
staunch blue bloods
Bannockburn commemorative
Sunday supplements
an incomer, summer bird
build up the borders
and feel all the more a tourist
a migrant here for August

MISCHARACTERISED HIEROGLYPHS

my body is a temple
daubed with mischaracterised hieroglyphs
a tatty atlas of wrong turns, mishaps
faded signs and crude paths, faddish reminders
of love dashed
and stuff
like a rudimentary time machine my armpit
is a window to the past
for the full picture, turn right at the nipple
follow the squiggle
Prince became a symbol
I'm a statement

a tipple, Dutch courage
a rose bloomed in a web of thumb
discreet, rosy-cheeked
a coquettish unicorn magicked up
on an unblemished bum
a blank canvass

there are more flowers
on my body than in a Chelsea bed
more words on my arm
than I have ever read
my thigh art, in the wrong light
looks like cellulite
but I am an outsider, queuing up
in tattoo parlance I am dangerous

I may look
like the colouring book
of a somewhat depressed chimp
but understand – this is the underground
alternative culture
I'm a rocker, a sailor, a footballer
someone from a boy band, six singles in
I'm a backpacker with a bad memory
a gift for Mother's Day

I am Sam Cam and Jen An
a rebel/ like Felicity Kendal
like Cheryl/ wild and free

one day I could be
David Dimbleby

UNDER MARDYKE WHARF *(FOR VID WARREN)*

under Mardyke Wharf
we urged his mouth
into big band sounds
an impromptu set
from the maestro's pit
baton-tongued, polyphonic spit
inching closer, astounded
he put his orchestra together
inhale: the rim shot, the hi-hat
exhale: a cymbal's steady groove
bring in the brass, a jazz scat
immaculate, percussive
a multitude of instruments
conjured from pockets
a track to pound the banks
of Banksy's backyard
take it to the bridge, to Isambard
unmoor Thekla, The Grain Barge
time adjusting to his rhythm
stopping, winding on to his beat
boxing bass drum, Cumberland Basin
throbs, the Avon vibrates, resonates
the effect of sound on water
wave upon wave upon wave

INDIANA JONES AND THE LAST SCHOOL MUG

on visiting a school, as a rule
remember *Indiana Jones
And The Last Crusade*

when selecting a cup –
choose wisely

simpler, plainer
one its own potter couldn't love
something with a carbuncle
a growth in its glaze
freebies and throwaways
remember – cups of Christ never advertise
local haberdashers

beware cracks, embedded rings
such vessels may not seem loved
but they are lived-in, their handles
gripped like the handrails of a boat
a hoop of hope, a life-ring keeping one afloat
through tempestuous Ofsteds
a call for heads, the pirate Gove
daydreams set sail in spiralling steam
a comforting watchtower
through every shipwrecked hour
marking time

never, ever
take one bearing a person's name
or a football crest
or David Hasselhoff

owners of these mugs
will hunt you like an elk
it matters not a jot you're a visiting poet
spreading joy and inspiration
drinking from that mug
is an open declaration of war

hell hath no fury like a maths teacher scorned
pursuing you, *Hunger Games*-style
through a fog of bloodlust
and caffeine deprivation
to where you sit, sipping, blithely unaware

these are not mugs –
they are all that's stopping the seams popping
and if one cannot believe in the sanctity of the mug
then maybe nothing is real
not algebra or Owen or rounders or soil

pass me that plain blue cup
the hideous one
at the back of the cupboard, never been touched
a seasonal mug out of season
no one wants to see Santa in June

don't arm me, don't alarm me
don't send me to that coliseum hall
with Mr Drip's favourite mug for all to see
do not allow my lips
to pucker that hot grenade
remember *Indiana Jones*
And The Last Crusade
and choose wisely
for my coffee

search among the crockery
beneath the collected bones of last year's dead poet
skull bashed in with repeated blows of a teaspoon
the swift athletic wrists of a PE teacher denied PG Tips
and unearth the mug that no one loves
blow from it sweet kiss curls of dust
fill its lumpy body with bitter blood
and I will raise that receptacle up
as if Christ himself had emblazoned it
with 'World's Greatest Messiah'
I need its fuel, its fire

and I need to tread
these halls
without a bounty on my head

I need my brew... pour me
please don't choose... poorly

BREAKWATER

let me be your breakwater
a block to stop the waves' nascent knock
soothe the savage seas that shock
sweep the world off its feet
sure, secure, steadied by this unwavering rock

let me paint the background
a thumb-flash splash
casting light to darkest path
a kaleidoscopic comet blazing you home
seek out my fire
when your soul desires, requires
something polychrome

let me be these words
whispered at your edges from afar
carry them about your day, taste their residue
pull them close to you
climb into their song when things overtake
may their rhythms carry you away

let me be your breakwater
if I cannot be the shore

let me paint the background
if I cannot claim the fore

let me be these words

if words are all I am

and nothing more

FEATHERED MASCOTS

ladies at Ascot in extravagant hats
feathered mascots of the purebred class
bringing mountainous peaks down to the flats
a flat track but no one told the heels
like the odds they're stacked, the real deal
4-1 shots and they'll keel
true to form, one falls at the first
2.15, lost the contents of her purse
boyfriend's going's even worse
had the shirt off his back
trampled in the turf, good to firm
backed a sure thing, pulled up lame
blinkered, betting's a mug's game
without drink on the brain
it's spelt out at a stroke – L-a-d / b-r-o-k-e
handicapped by the tote, on his knees
he frantically flips discarded slips
before an emptying grandstand
she's hitching home, bust heels in hand
this morning's fancied
come evening, also-rans

BALACLAVA OF MIRRORS

strobe lights probe, highlight the disrobed
spot-lit white-hot in mirrored globes
on the dance floor, a molten redhead glows
her sweat-wet dress hemmed with picket fences
hatchbacks scrunched into impotent bits
magnetised, I hang off her like a mobile
useless feet dangling, desperate to impress
dancing nonetheless, limbs depressed
and jerking like a push-puppet giraffe
'save your breath,' she mouths, 'you're not my type'
I'm coming on like a bad song, a floor-clearer

'first let me say' (I begin to her back)
'what appalling taste you have in men
furthermore – how many "your types" are still on the scene?
haven't they all eroded / exploded / disappointed / disappeared?'

spinning, a smile licks at the corner of her lip gloss
'you must know,' she intones
'I only want someone who doesn't want me
when I find him, I grind him down, turn him around
until guess what – he's loopy, wants me desperately
wants until he's anathema to me, a kiss – acidic
that beautiful face nothing but a bashed tapestry
of ugly lines and uneven symmetry'

I look up to her, reflected
in the mirrored ceiling
cool liquid rushes to meet those lips
she sips and I'm agog
what eclipses the chase
the countdown to the first date
the rate at which the world dissipates
all sound ceasing, nothing exists
air collapsing into kiss
everything heightened / taut / tightened
before the inevitable slide
into that where's-this-going line of questioning
compromises that please no one
resentment festering

that first meet – it's not you, it's not them
it's your highlight reels running simultaneously –
your Best of Life
like cricket on the news condensed into two minutes
of wicket-taking, extravagant strokes
it's only in the real-time grind
you find it's all no-balls
and bad light stopping play
constantly skirting round feelings
seldom feeling round skirt

in the epicentre, where epic enters
clinging on as everything burns, inwardly turns
records swamp into wax
Booker T, Otis in stacks
we're showboating
for that next person in which to bask
reflected back all witty and shimmering
the realest fakes on the make
all guileless give for take

at hers she makes me wear a balaclava of mirrors
through a join in the plating
I see her wink at herself as her orgasm nears
she shouts her name
and I scream mine until the neighbours hear
and start to complain

later she consents to wear the balaclava
we're moving like liquid
rhythmical and fluid
uncontainable, unrestrainable
I look into those eyes just in time
to catch myself mouthing 'I love you'
and I smile

finally this is it

SWINDISNEY

In 2009, Walt Disney World (Florida) invited bids for a UK twin. Swindon won.

once upon a time
Walt Disney World
was but half a world
a princess without a prince
so, missing a twin, a link
(alone and towered)
the Magic Kingdom
lowered its hair down
to Swindon

if you've ever been
you'll know it's the same
Swindon is Disneyland in all but name
a utopia on a modest hill built
the American Dream made Wilts

there's more magic in its roundabout
that mesmerising ballet
of hatchbacks and coupés
the coup de grâce of town planning gone cuckoo
than with Dumbo or Baloo
and if you tire of the Magic Roundabout
there's plenty more roundabouts
round abouts

the town boasts some of the most
spectacular rectangular buildings in Europe
what a view from the library, a floor up
who needs Splash Mountain
with MECA as a backdrop?

the Americans are coming in droves
lured by old-fashioned glamour
Billie Piper, Melinda Messenger, Diana Dors
they're riding round in four-by-fours
exploring Penhill, Pinehurst, Park North

snapping away excitedly in their cars
the legacy of Brunel and GWR
Isambard, the great inventor
better linked now with a shopping centre

the cinema that became a Wetherspoons
the Groves spirit merchant's that became a Wetherspoons
The Sir Daniel Arms that became
The Sir Daniel Arms
Wetherspoons

Typhoon Lagoon cannot compete
with the pedestrianised splendour of Regent Street
American tourists getting used
to using their feet
to see the sights of New Disney

more glittering than Cinderella's ball
strike the clock atop the town hall
flora, flora on the living wall
Swindon, you be the fairest
of them all

MERMAID

I've no recollection of the night in question
I told the judge evenly, the CCTV
damned undoubtedly, us
rowing at the seaside, the holidaymakers
bounding in to testify, treasured memories
kept alive

I downed a glass of water
an action the media repeatedly analysed
and analysed though couldn't quite decide
whether to treat as guilt or pride
my mouth bone-dry
from the airless courtroom

had I merely buried her, playfully
in the cold dark sand and forgotten?
driven home alone that night, oblivious

her a mermaid returned to the sea
that sharp, serrated tongue cutting
at the waves like a wicked fin

SHADOW-BOXING SNOWFLAKES

blond youngster maybe eight
shadow-boxing snowflakes
each stands in the way
of his title hopes
pins one with a low jab
tight up against the shelter ropes
a second lands on his tongue
'what's my name?!' he taunts its tingle
a single swift and brutal swallow
another challenger slain, gone

come morning there will be a thick white canvas
commuters standing awed and helpless
but this first fall, so unannounced and small
makes the boy dance, entranced
flick a fast right deep, distributing weight
a line settling on his knuckles
cloaks where the punches scrape
towelling white collar working bomber nape

fall in all comers, float, fight
give out boxer, all your might
a combination, two left, one right
rock it, shock the snow
bring about a knockout blow
a muffled yet conclusive bell
a soft-shoe shuffle, the victory yell

confetti fell! ticker tape! the train
appears, nears, as it brakes
he hears the acclaim, the fame
the echoed chanting of his name
great wheels squeal steel applause

and the bigger it comes
the harder, still, it falls

CALL IT DUTY

sh-sh-sh-shoot me
call it duty
put that phallic/ metallic/ weaponry
to my head
reboot me

this feels unreal, stage-managed
for the flat screen
patrols scrolling through the same scenes
ketchup reds, Technicolor greens
overshot, the tired fatigues
props from a Hollywood lot

we're here to keep the peace
but you can't keep
what you've never seen
enemies in trees
the only peace they want
is a piece of me
when did I last sleep?
sleep is for the weak
must be weeks
break the programming

every step a command
urged on by unseen hands
strange how the word *pacifist*
terminates in *fist*
untwist that taloned hate
straighten as a flower
aim toward the sun
depetal your digits
one by one
let go the gun

did I sign up for this?
some dumb kid
swayed by snake-oil recruiters
and a flashy vid

a small town where no one
amounts to spit
go see the world
and shoot at it
drafted?
deemed fit and able
by a cabal of grey men
massed around a table
who wouldn't put
their own sons forward
to get ordered
captured
tortured

fighting a country
of which I know nothing
for a country
I no longer believe in
one that would rather
change the channel
than deal with the grieving
when everything you love
is everything you hate
everything you love is hate

AWOL
free of control – consoled
I stroll down
bombed-out streets
in civilian gear
finger hovering on a trigger
somewhere near
you think you can just play with life?
a dozen shootings before breakfast time
wipe the redcurrant jam from the knife?
step outside, throw the curtains wide

Columbine
Virginia Tech

Newtown
where next?
not in my name

sh-sh
it's just a game

just a game

DEFECTING DANIEL

she began her approach as I began my set
moving like a post office queue
one shuffle nearer the stage
for every forty words leaving the page
I was riding the last wave of applause
heading for the green-room doors
when finally she reached me
a hunched-up scrunched-up speck
in a voice like a haunted accordion
she proclaimed me the new Daniel O'Donnell

had I been that bad?
I mean, I had things on my mind
a cold coming
but I didn't feel particularly... off
I was turning inwards, shrinking
sinking into a thin-skinned artistic funk
when, gradually, and this will come as a shock, folks
it started to dawn this was a compliment
and not any compliment but *the* compliment
sure, it's not wholly transferrable –
I'm a poet, he's whatever he is...
'if I was sixty years younger...' she croaked
winking, catching even her face off-guard
she looked like she was trying to swallow a bunk bed

this is how I met Misty Seabird
great-great-gran super fan
Misty, she's 103, her face a comic scowl
her barnet's a regatta of spatchcocked owl hairpieces
a lifeless curl lowers Rapunzel-like
to a Pomeranian slightly smaller than she
affixed permanently to her sometime-functioning knee
this dog, it doesn't think so highly of me

Misty, she's seen Daniel 106 times
has his autograph on nine of her cardies
and a restraining order for unspecified crimes
she's now defected to me – she's my number-one fan

she's crocheted my face into a shopping bag
it looks like Sharon Osborne but she swears it's me
poor lamb, she's got cataracts and can hardly see
her knitting hand is but a claw
the bag gave out one day in Asda
stretched my face with bread and pork
fruit and veg poking through
made me look like Carmen Miranda
morphing into Mickey Rourke

poor Misty, old habits die hard
three days before my gig above a pub
she's outside in her fold-up chair
rain comes, wind stirs, but she won't be deterred
the landlady brings out coffee and scampi fries
it's a running battle just to keep her alive
I try to get her to come inside
I'm only expecting thirty, the room takes sixty easy
but she wants to be first in officially
sit at the front, ear trumpet, double gin
take my picture on an old box Brownie with powder flash
it went off in Stockport, dislocated the 'tache
part of my beard ensemble, blew up in my face in Hull
I was known for a month as One-Eyebrow Ash

Misty's heard every one of my poems
but given her goldfish memory
every word seems brand new
between me and you, I think she thinks I'm Dick Emery
for she keeps saying, 'ooh, you are awful... but I like you'

having such a devoted fan
makes me question the commitment of others
those casual sorts that catch me once a year
or somewhere near
people like you...

when did you last tattoo my likeness on to your shin?
ink whole stanzas of mine into your skin?

shave 'Slinky Espadrilles' into the side of your dog?
when did you last sit outside my window in the pouring rain
with a sodden cardboard heart bearing my name
– answer honestly
when did you last watch nothing
but my YouTube videos for seventy-two hours straight?
you're lying – you've never done that
what do you mean you don't know all my poems off by heart
even that ropey one about capybaras?
it's not good enough

I haven't the time for fair-weather
prawn-sandwich-munching dilettantes
you're useless to me, dead weight
shape up, soldier, buck up
your backing or you're a goner
left behind, only fit to follow
Daniel O'Donnell

A BATTLE OF QUILLS

I walked into a darkness only my mood could match/ still,
save for the feathery thrum of insects, born blind as new love/
sound cowered, trees, clouds as if there were a line they dared
not cross/ I pushed on into this darkness like a sleepwalker/
pressing against nothing until my hands struck cold stone/ it
was a bar, a twisted knotted den

in this bar, a man said he could write me under the table/ and
taking a pen from his jacket he began composing mountains/
puppeteering them from the page/ far grander than any I'd
ever conceived, they rose with ferocity/ sneered down upon
the homesteads of the wealthy/ each with swimming pools of
azure blue, rectangular or curved as fish around acres of garden/
tearing ever upwards until one plump peak pricked Pluto as if it
were an olive/ snow fell from his pen in great cursive flurries/
landing as seas, roaring and raging/ battering the steely flesh
of trawlers/ coursing out far past the breakwater of the margin

he wrote me into a corner/ wrote me a question mark as a crook,
hooked around my neck/ bayonet pen poised to scrawl pink ink
at the ridges of my ribcage/ 'what?' he challenged, 'no fight?'/
– there were exits, I noted/ holes in his plot/ just big enough
to poke a biro through/ to create/ to shape/ – to escape/ but
my pen was hungover/ it hacked up a puddle of drunken black
blood I can only describe as beetle carnage/ I wished to duck for
rainbows/ pluck the sails from windmills/ but I was like a child,
muted by trauma/ storing up words like a typewriter ribbon

the shadow of the chandelier cast a spider on the ceiling/ it's just
a feeling but it's building/ a deep seed germinating/ the barflies
sat like our excesses/ like plot devices/ the coat stand eyed me
like an undercover cop/ I felt it taking hold/ two bluebottles
mate in a small theatre, oblivious to cast or audience/ a sound
engineer picks up faint frenzied buzzing/ in a busy restaurant in
Lima, a new mother lactates through her blouse/ a waiter with
comic book stubble, saucers of sweat under his arms, in dropping
a plate surprises a child into letting go a balloon which rises and
taps at the skylight/ this makes the waiter sad/ straining for a
freedom it's never had/ I am that balloon, he thinks/ ...I felt it
building/ ...I felt it taking hold

yet for every loophole, he wrote a clause/ for every manhole, a cover/ I was scribbling parachutes and ejector seats/ pen and sheet meeting fevered and desperate like illicit lovers/ I was Roger Bannister/ Houdini/ I was framed by a scrawl – mine to study/ 'I wish to write with abandon,' it began/ 'thrash open the nib, flood the page with civilisations/ widen my mouth thick as a mighty river/ have the words spray, cascade/ before distilling to a single drop/ an ungainly man vainly hangs on to his toupee/ as the wind whips through his soft top coupé/ do I write because I'm a loner/ or am I a loner because I write?'/ and there it stopped/ I saw he was a slat on a blind twitching slowly/ next an old man looking at me curiously/ his eyes strangely pretty/ he sported genuinely arresting trousers/ his face a zoo on a wet day

what if I wrote of magic?/ what then?/ all this oneupmanshit/ misplaced anger/ mean-spiritedness/ why not be the life raft/ the up-draught/ the crash cart/ a star to steer by?

he pencilled himself a dragon for a mouthpiece/ across the sky, it vaingloriously scorched these words: 'if that isn't the mealiest bunkum I've yet heard/ I wouldn't use a book of yours to right a wonky table/ you're no rival – but say you're right and we unite/ draw this venom from my face/ make flesh the taste/ earliest man, worn to sand/ caricatures of coal dredged up from the land/ onward, waste ground to waste ground/ deep prospecting/ chip down for the gold/ tap at the specks of black that eat at your soul/ a blanket of catkins Mexican wave alongside the 8.17 to Manchester/ a giant sack of cat/ frost-white-fronted, tabby-backed/ flops on to the lap of a retired optometrist/ do I write because I'm never alone/ when the words align?'

days die/ the word survives/ faces fade, age/ ideas pass away/ the page remains/ caught in time/ notarise/ diarise/ invent it/ document it/ I happen upon a light/ a sight my eyes swallow whole/ the setting just right – dry kindling and a clearing, slash and burn/ just as the light turns a brilliant gold/ I take up my pen/ corral it as it grows, takes hold/ slip it oxygen, gargle paraffin/ I'm fire-treating, flame-growing/ I throw back my head/ I'm fire-eating/ that moment, I'm flame-throwing